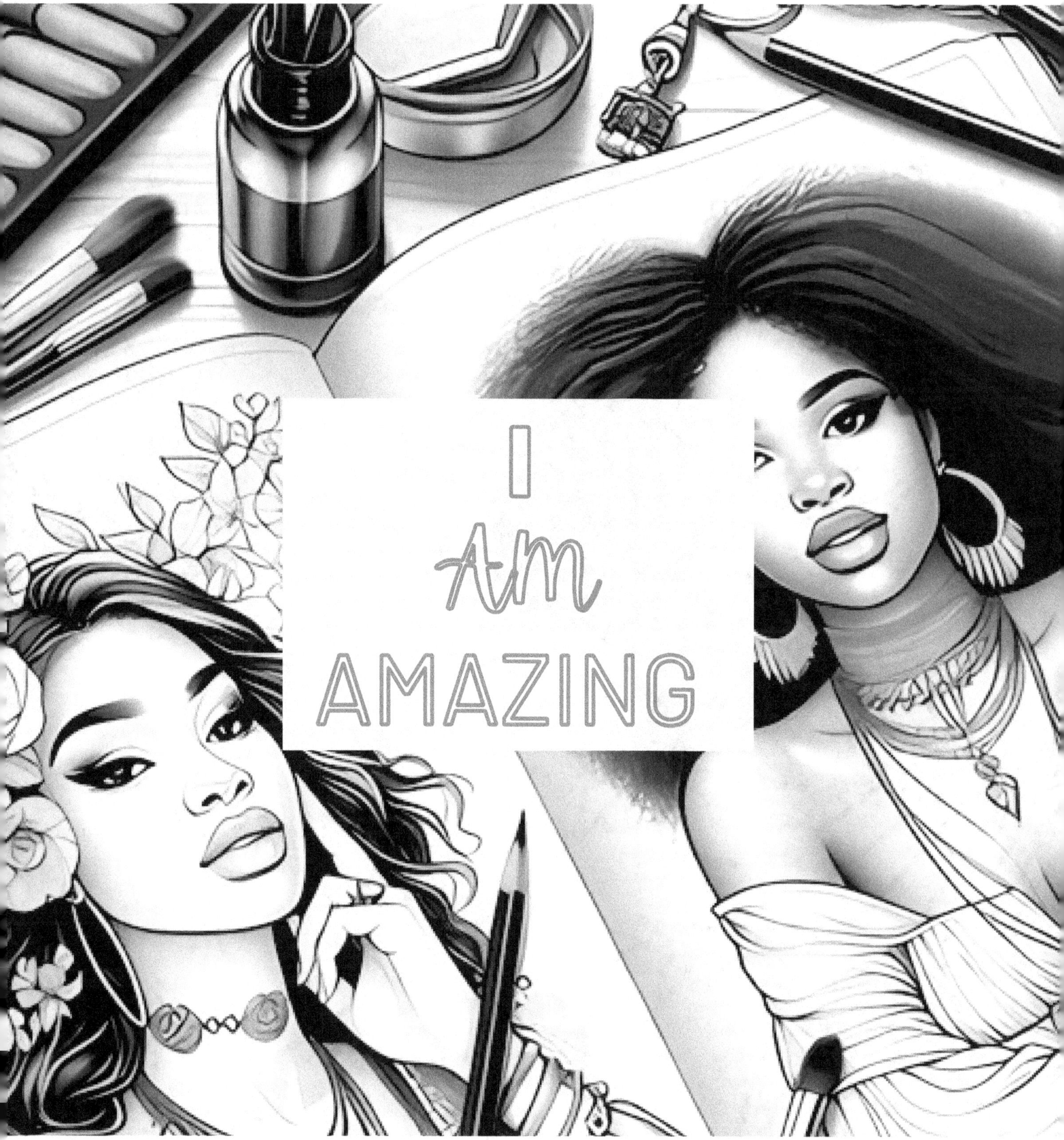
I
Am
AMAZING

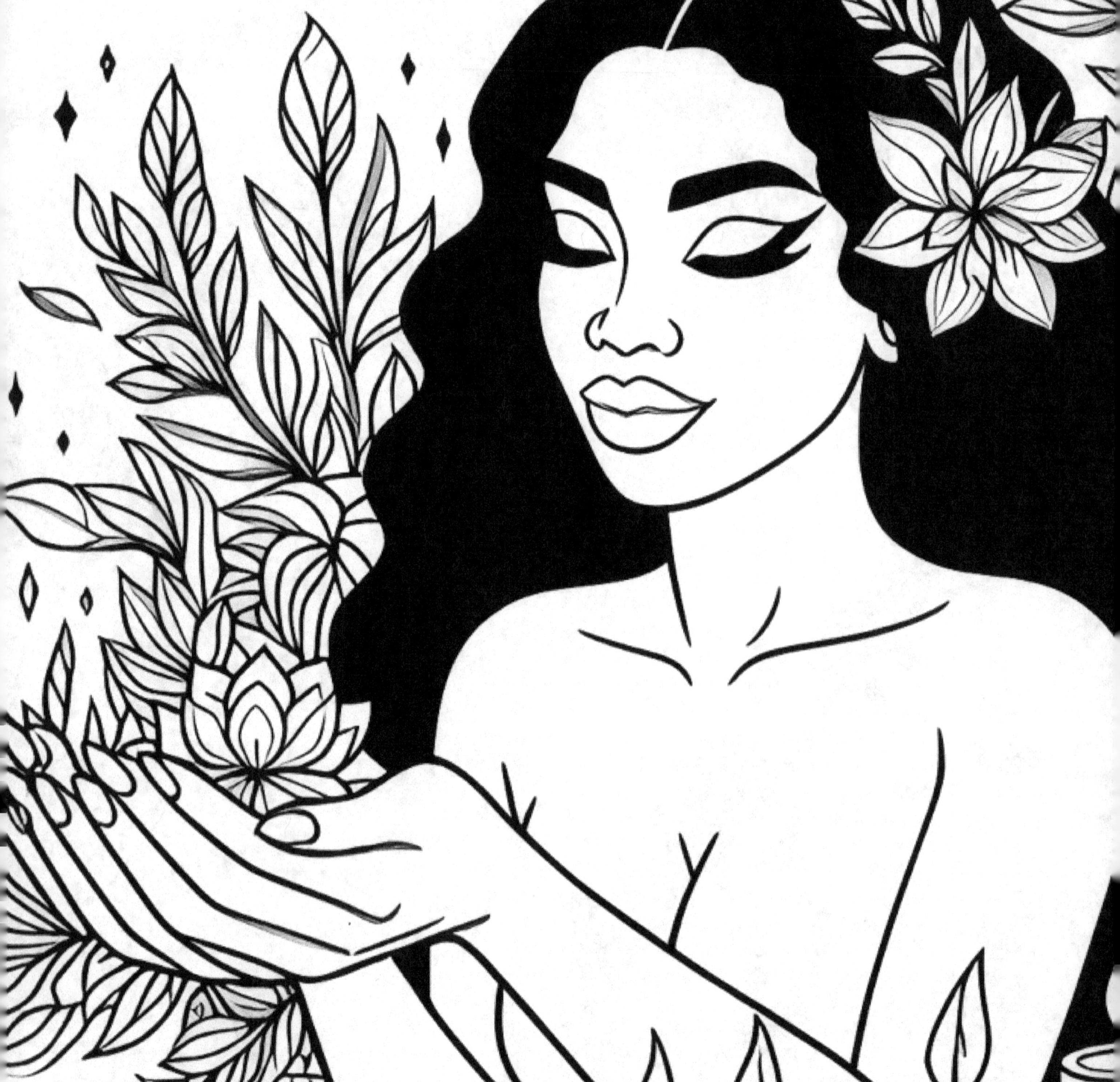

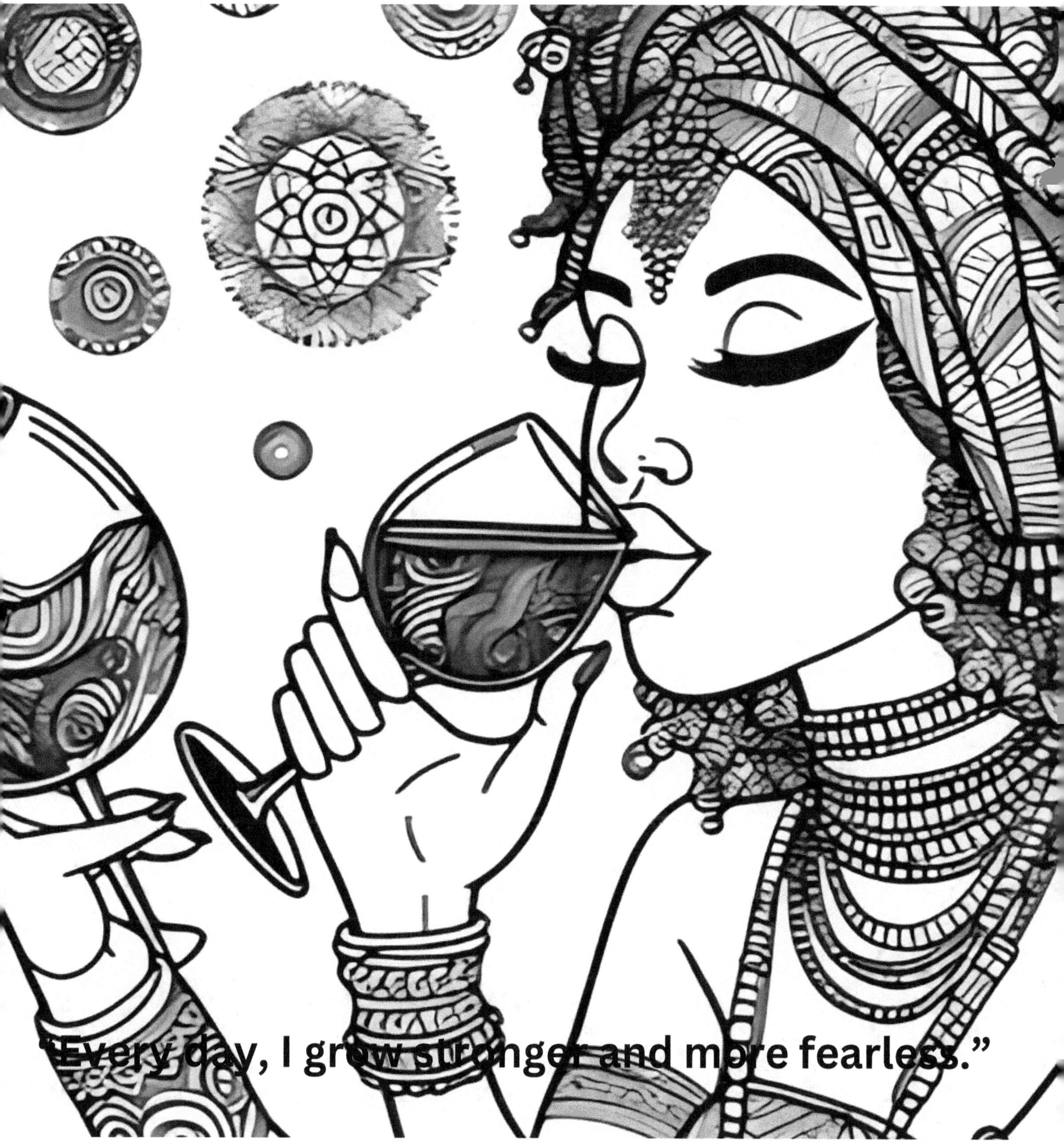

"Every day, I grow stronger and more fearless."

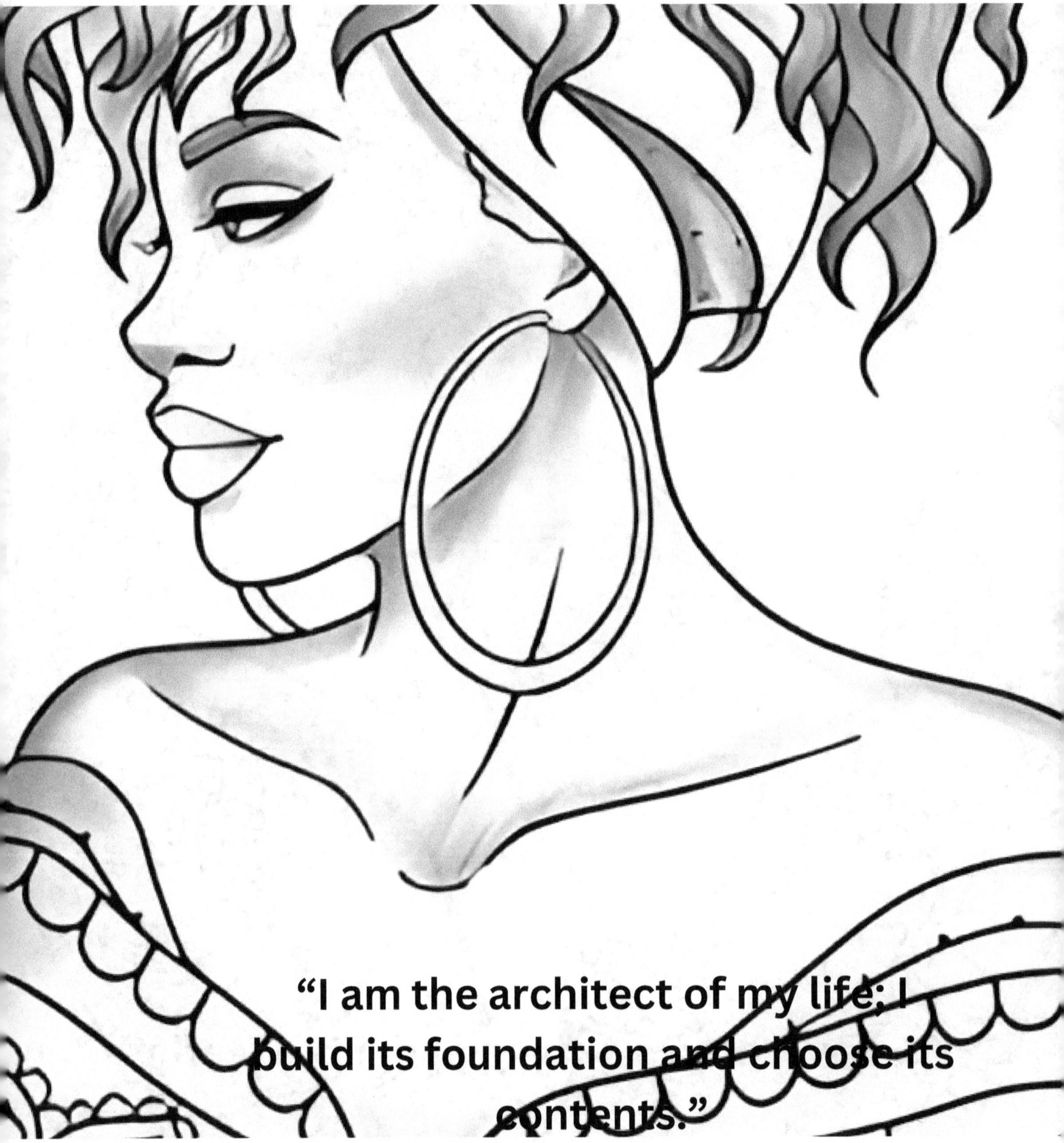

"I am the architect of my life; I build its foundation and choose its contents."

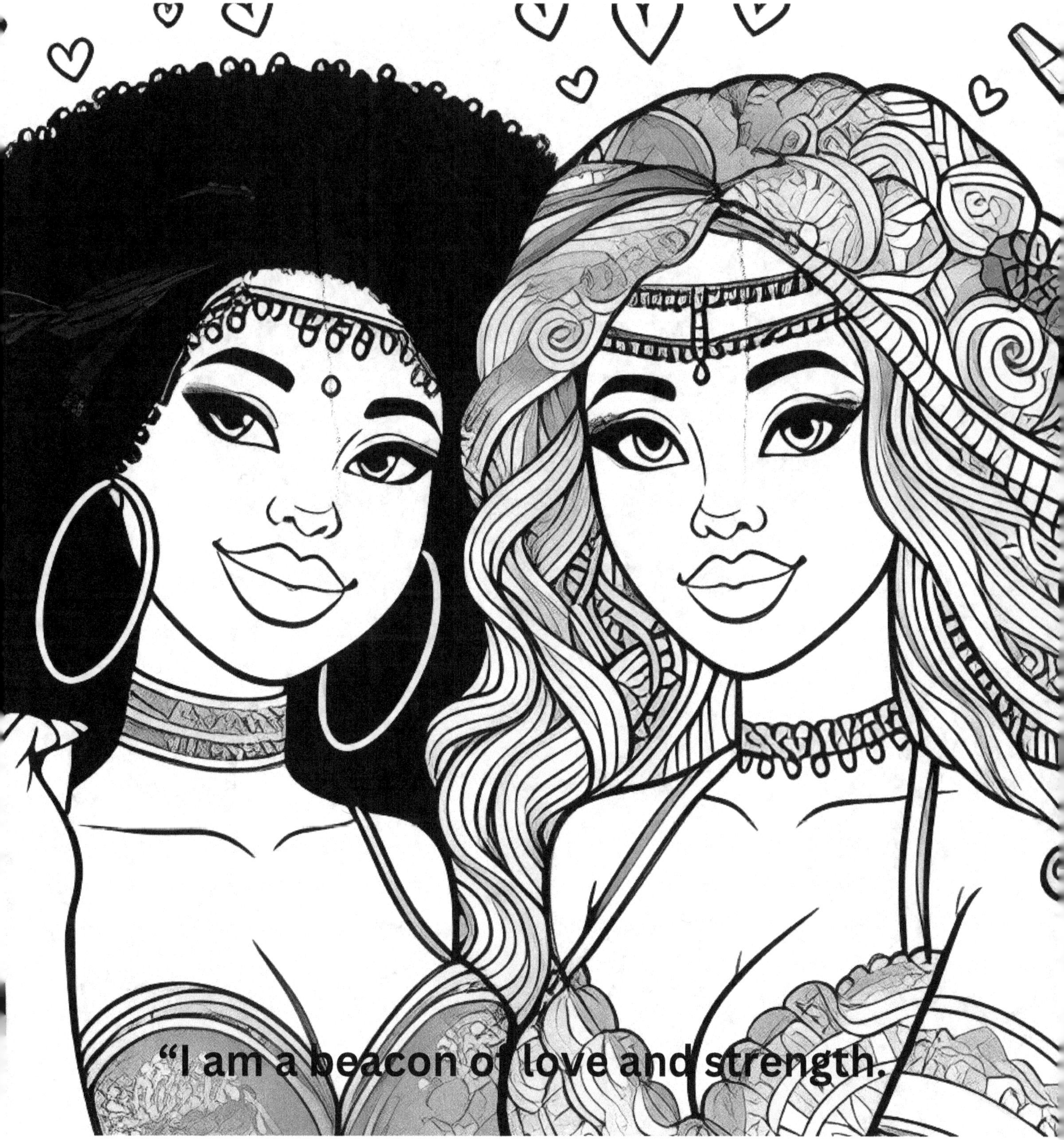
"I am a beacon of love and strength.

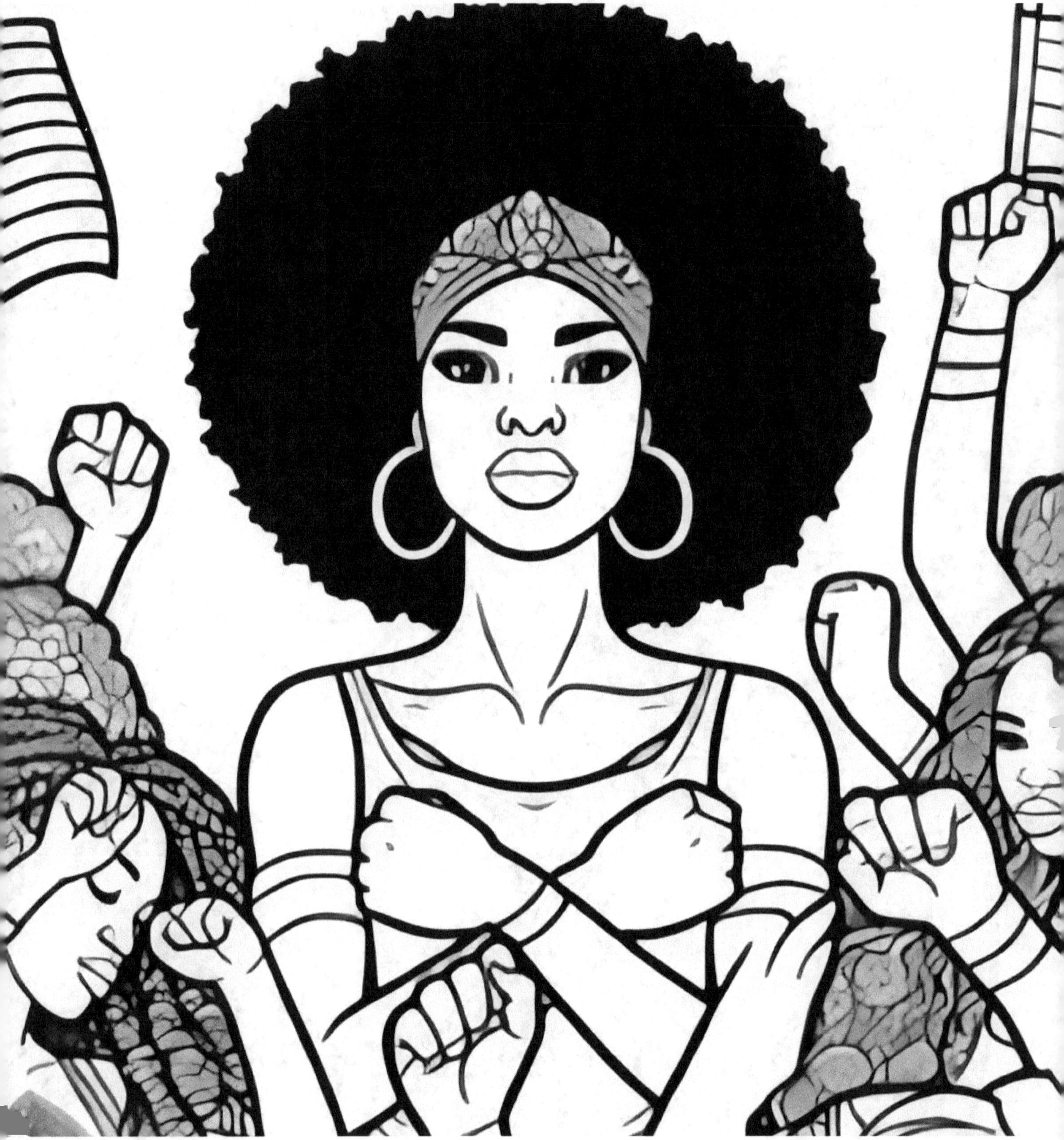

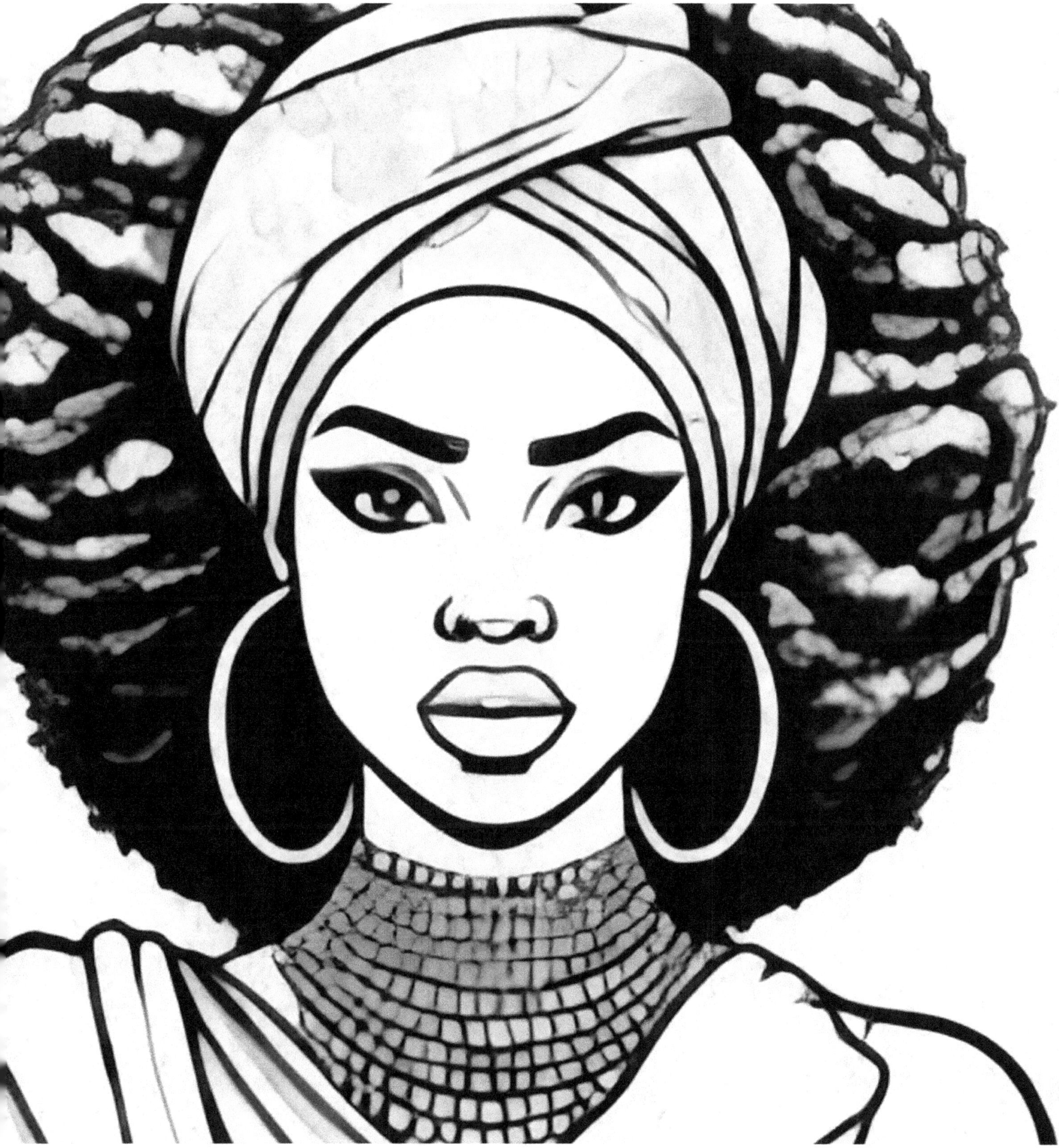

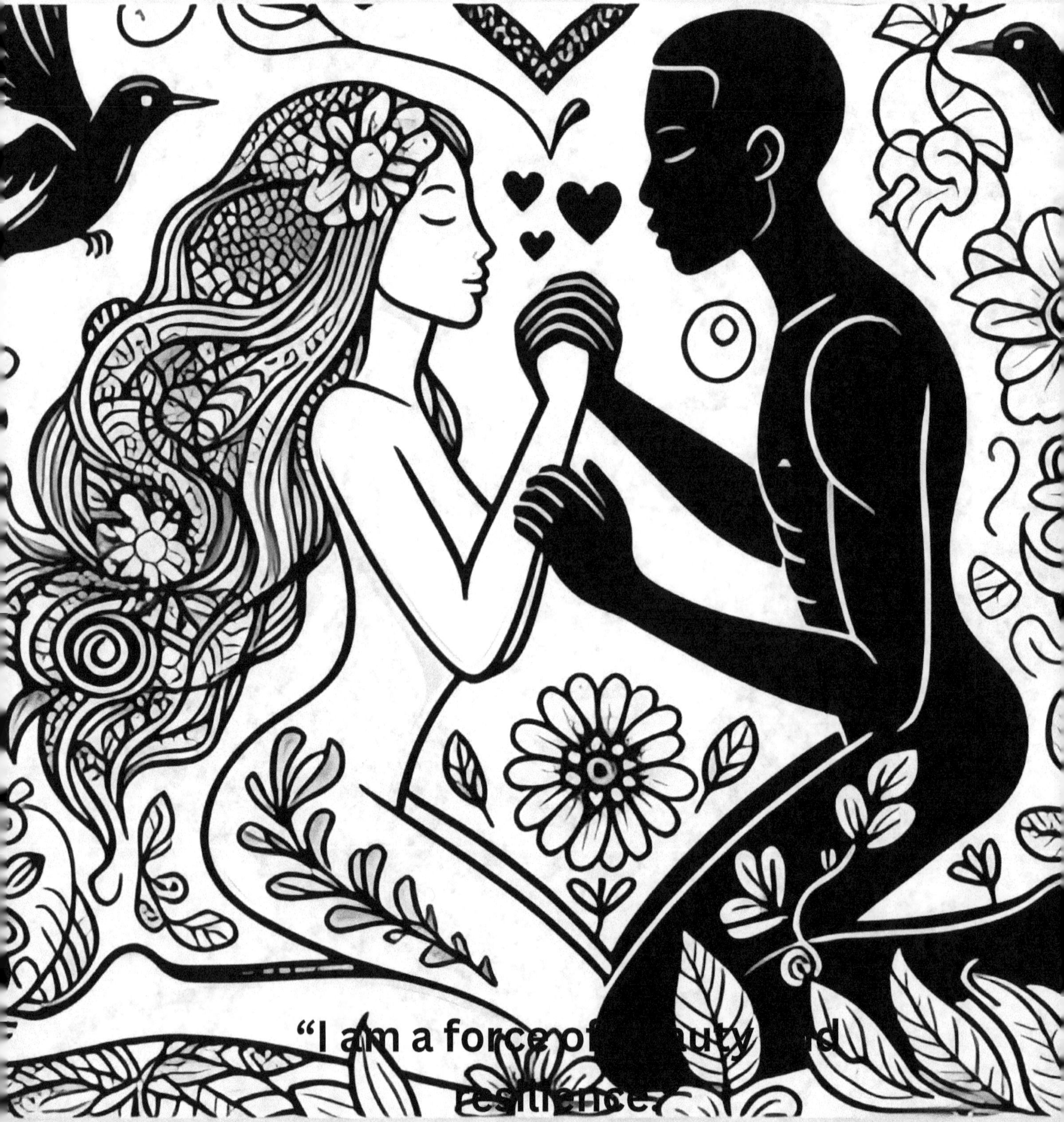

“I am a force of beauty and resilience.”

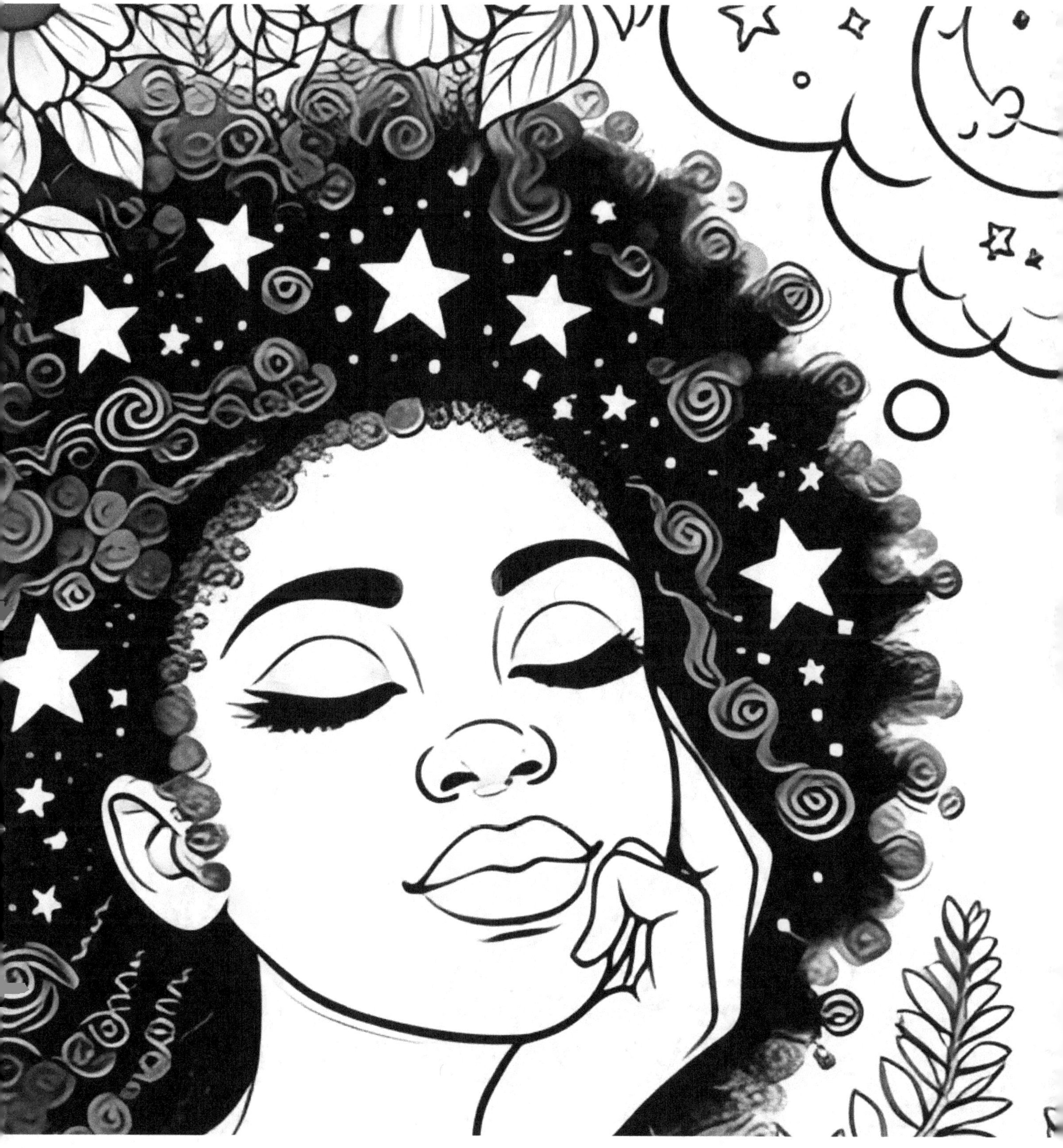

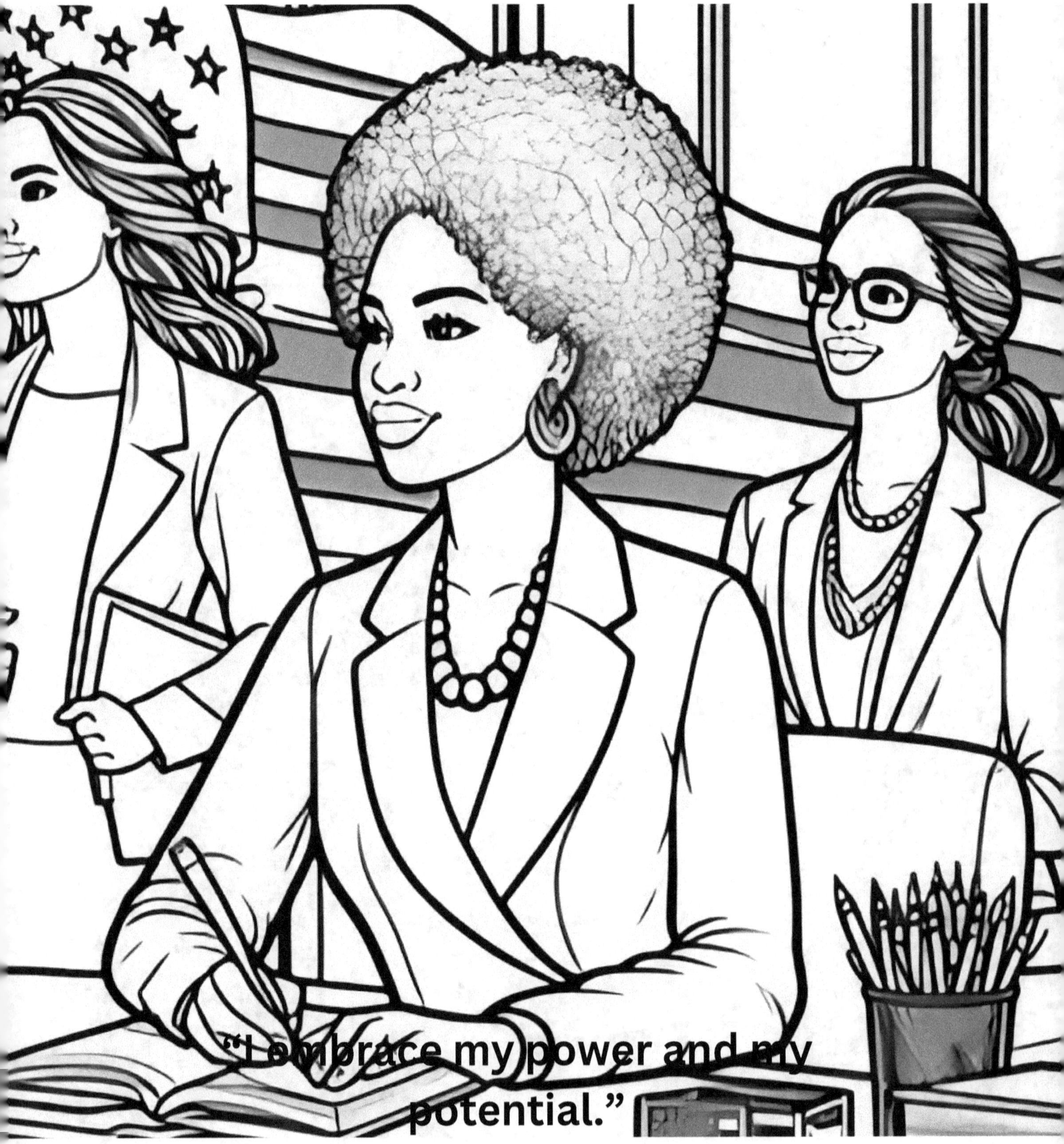
“I embrace my power and my potential.”

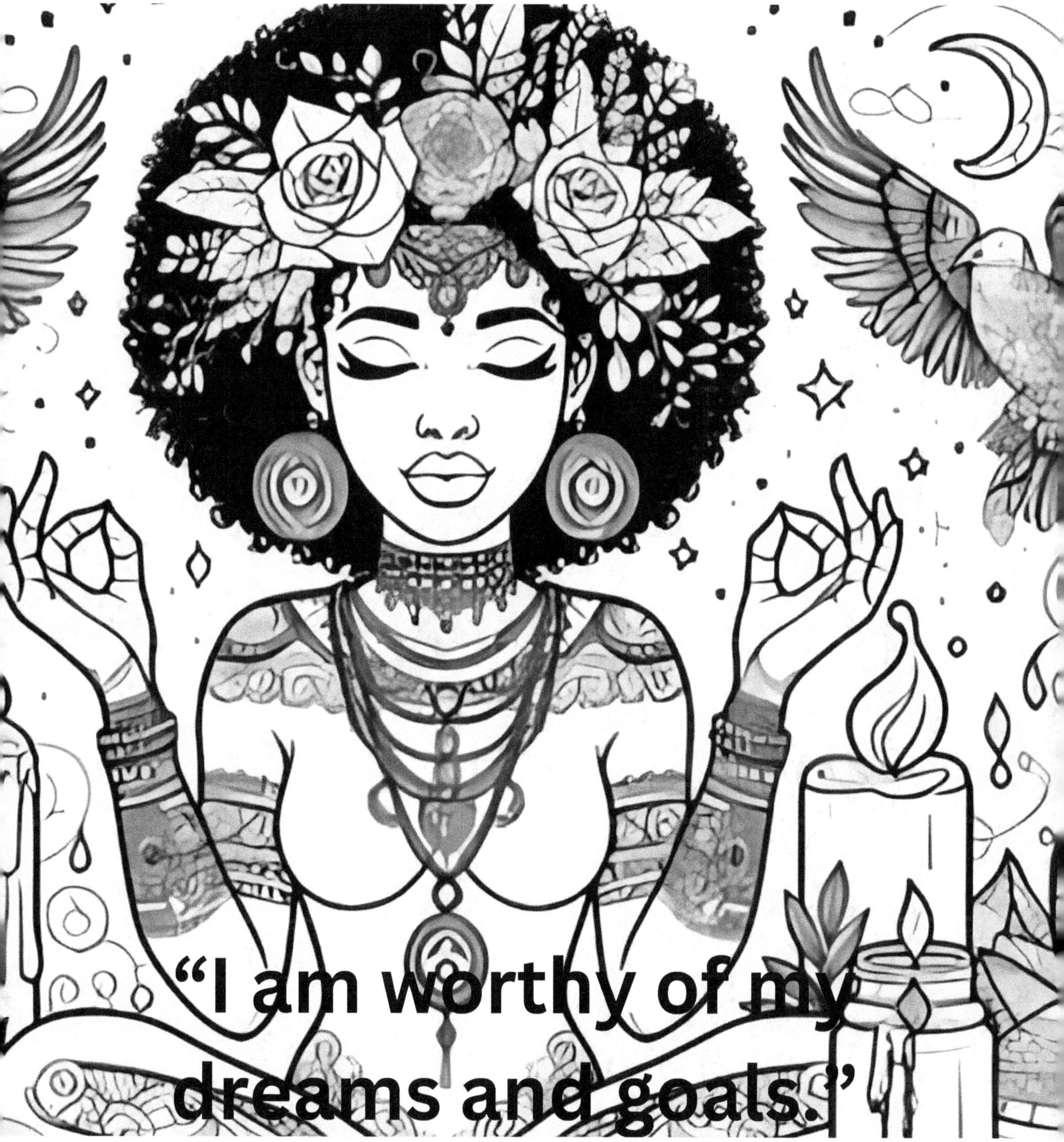
“I am worthy of my
dreams and goals.”

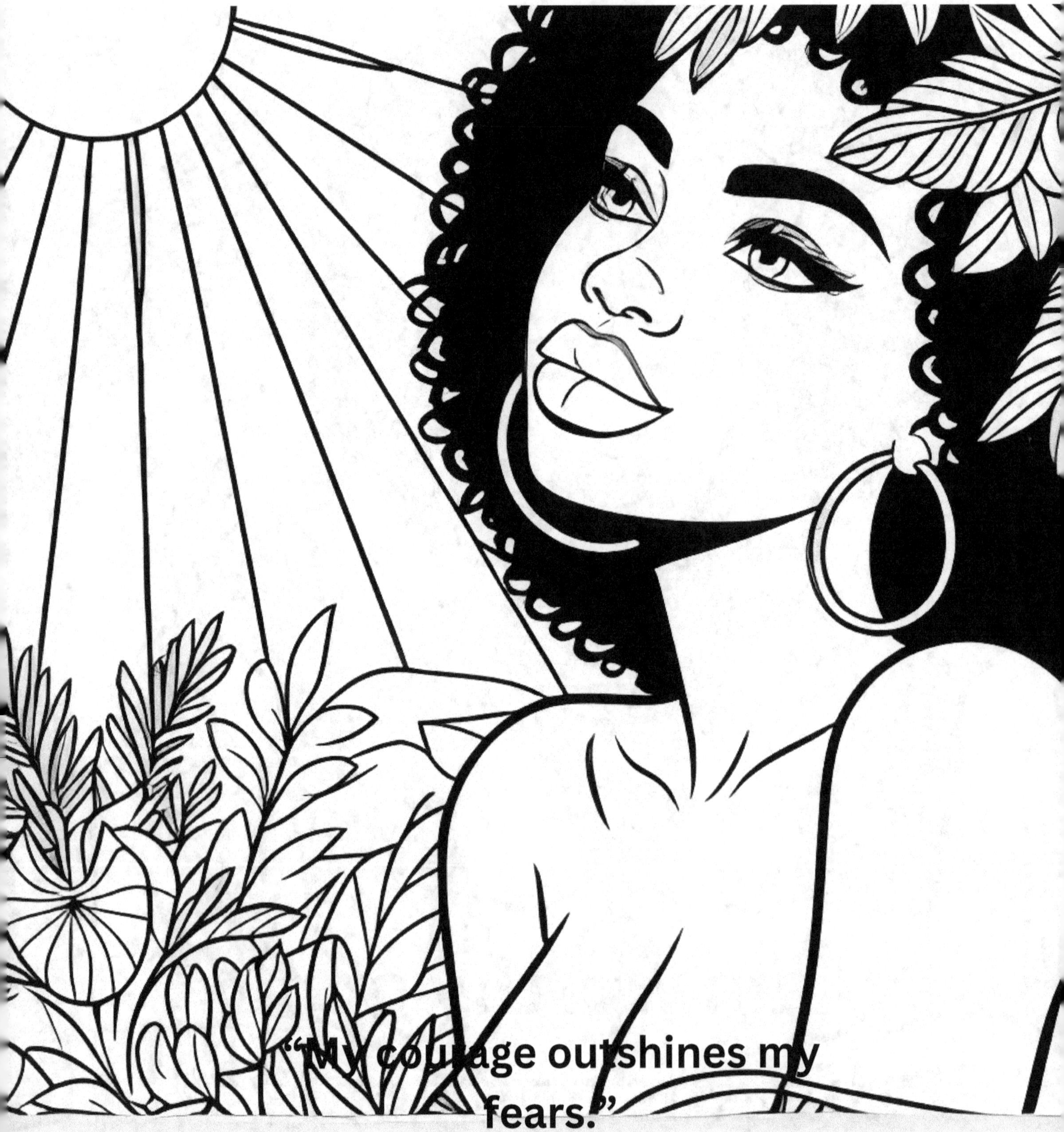

“My courage outshines my fears.”

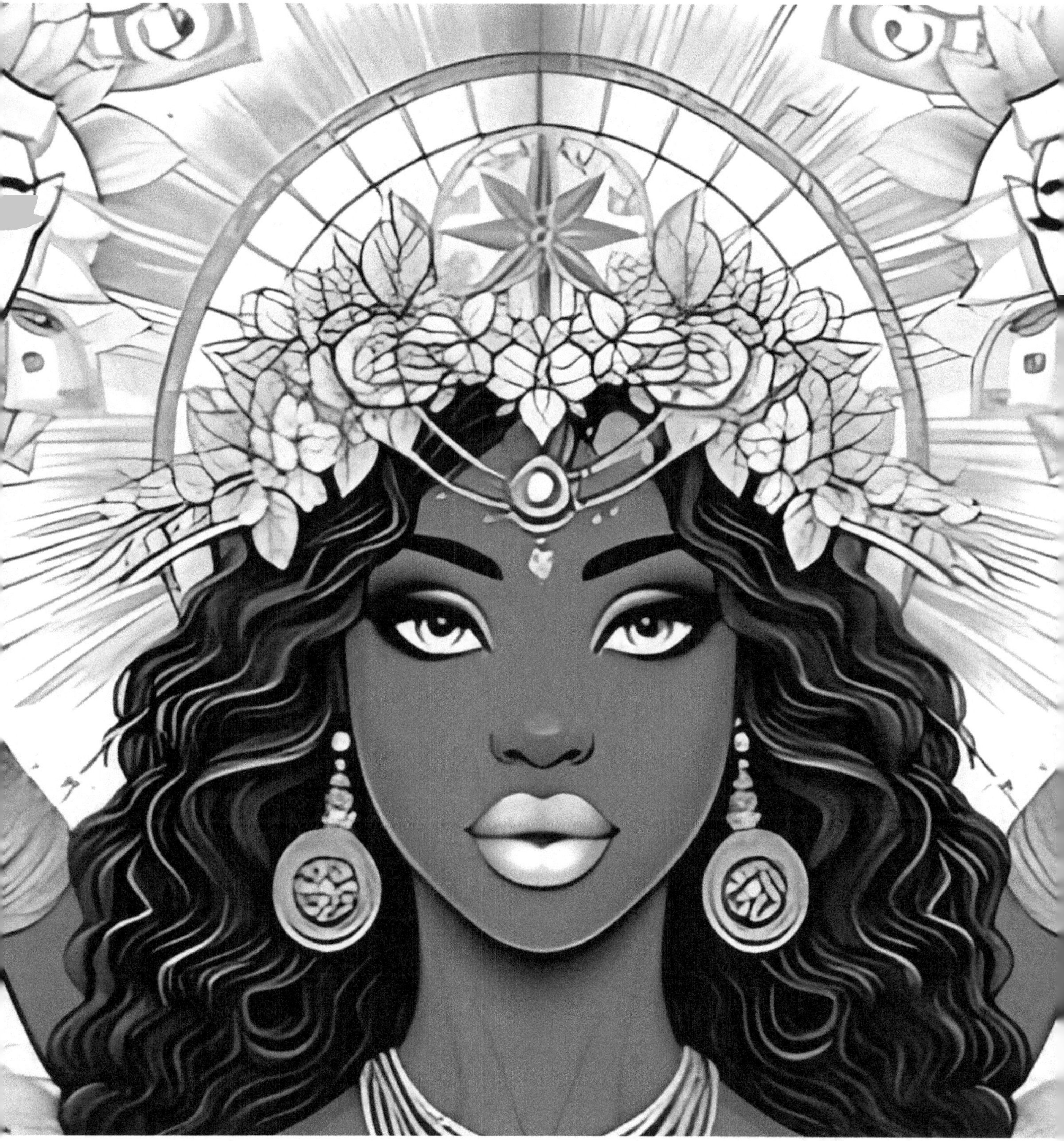

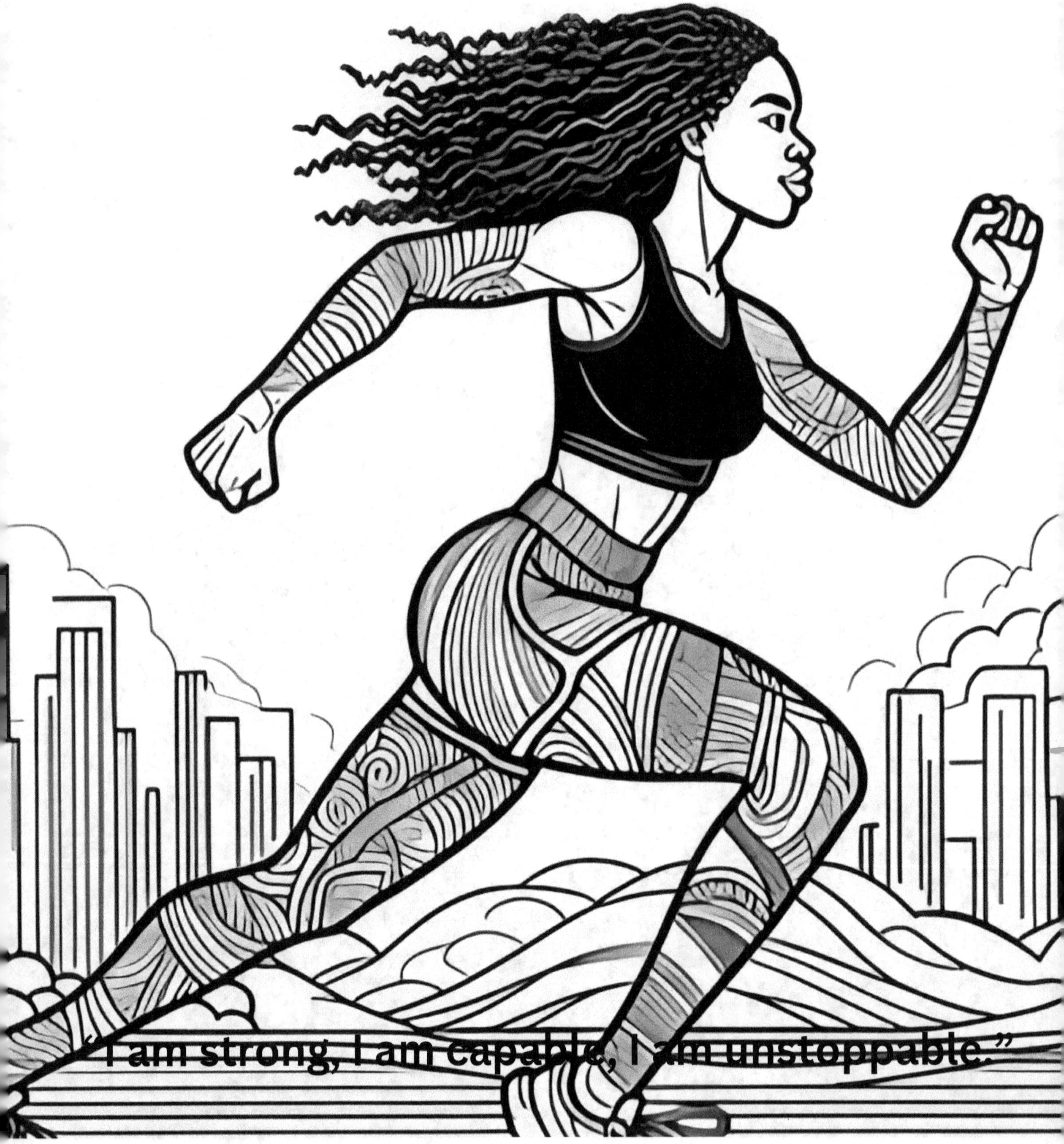

"I am strong, I am capable, I am unstoppable."

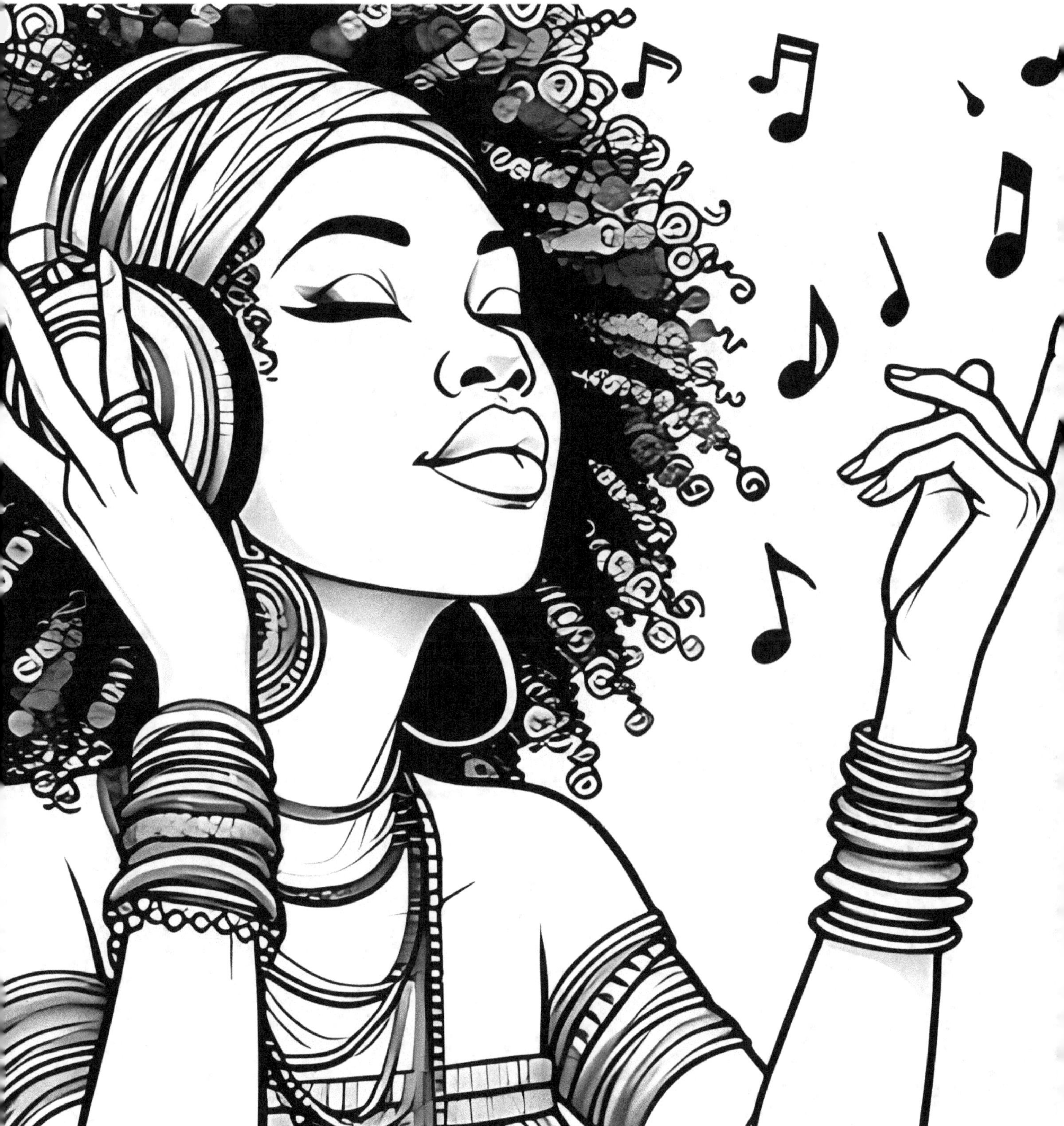

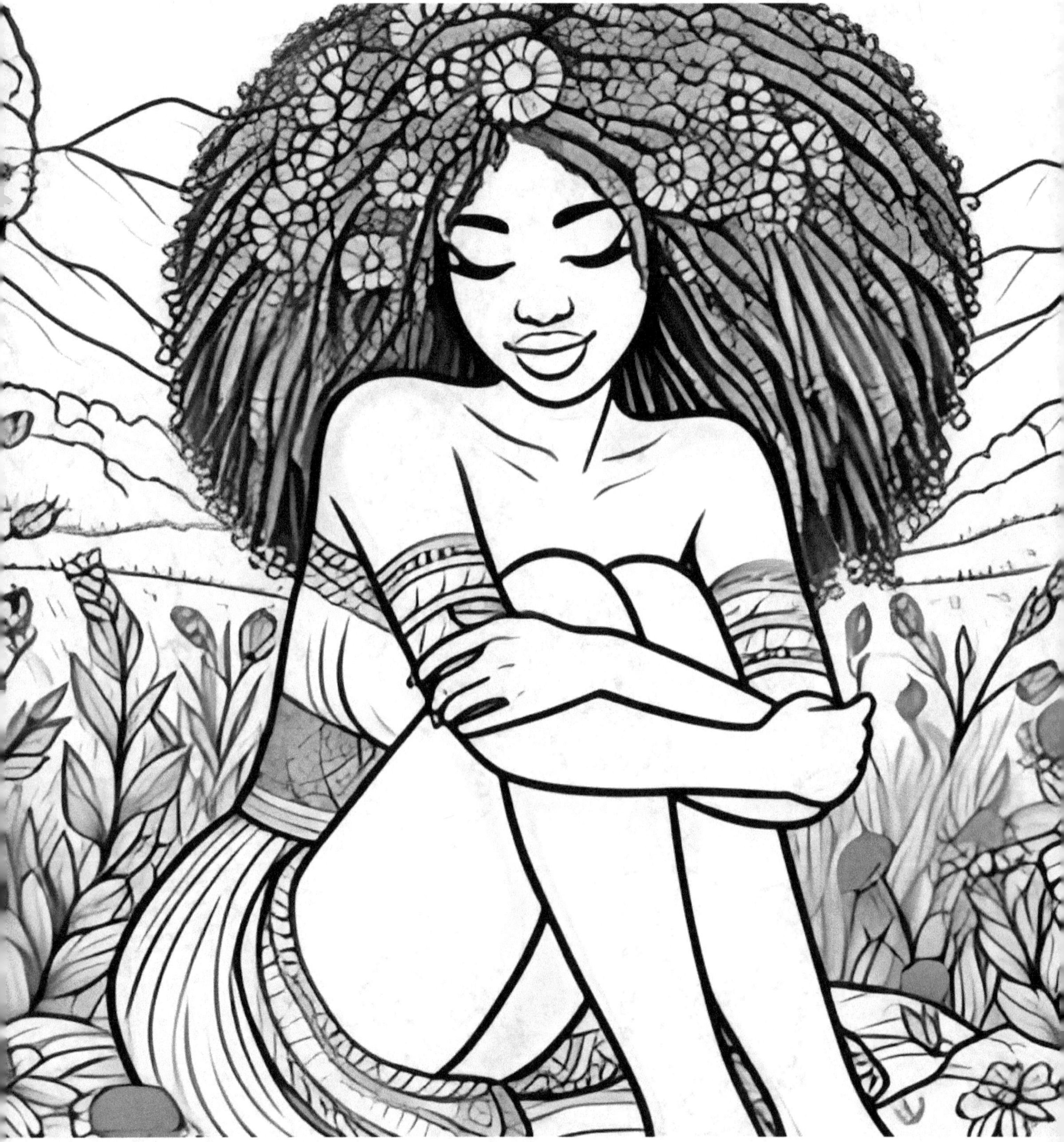

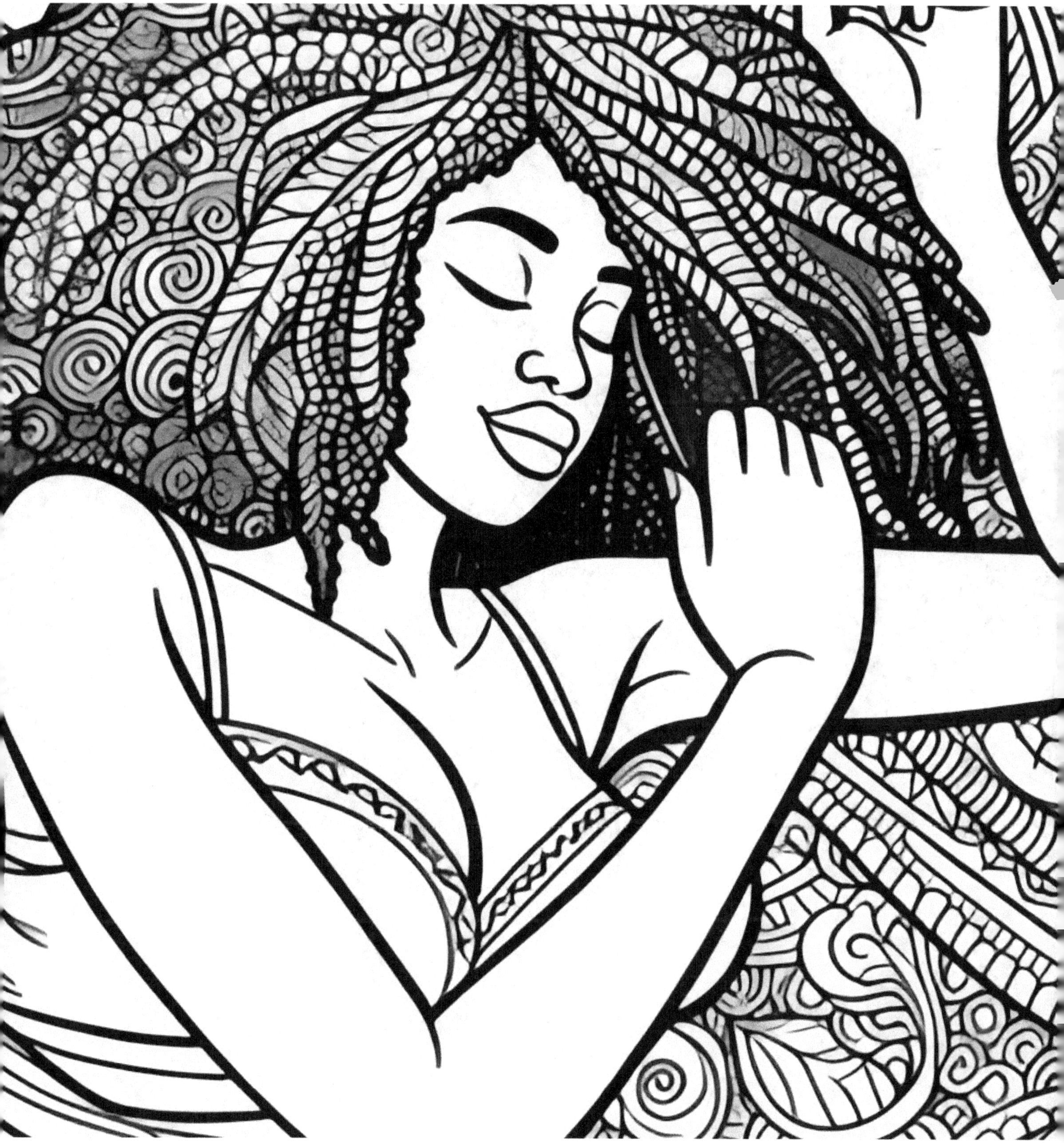

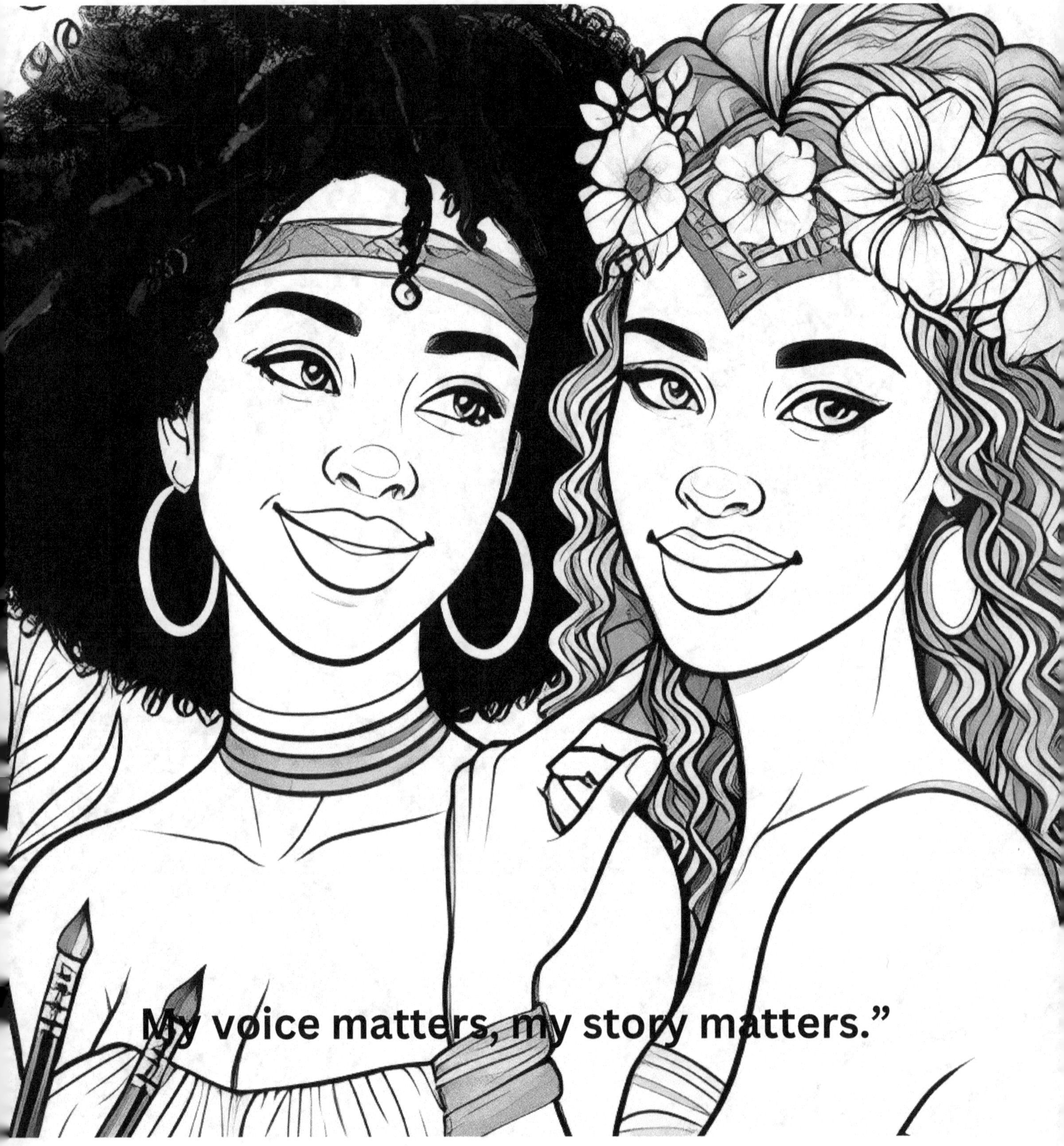
My voice matters, my story matters.”

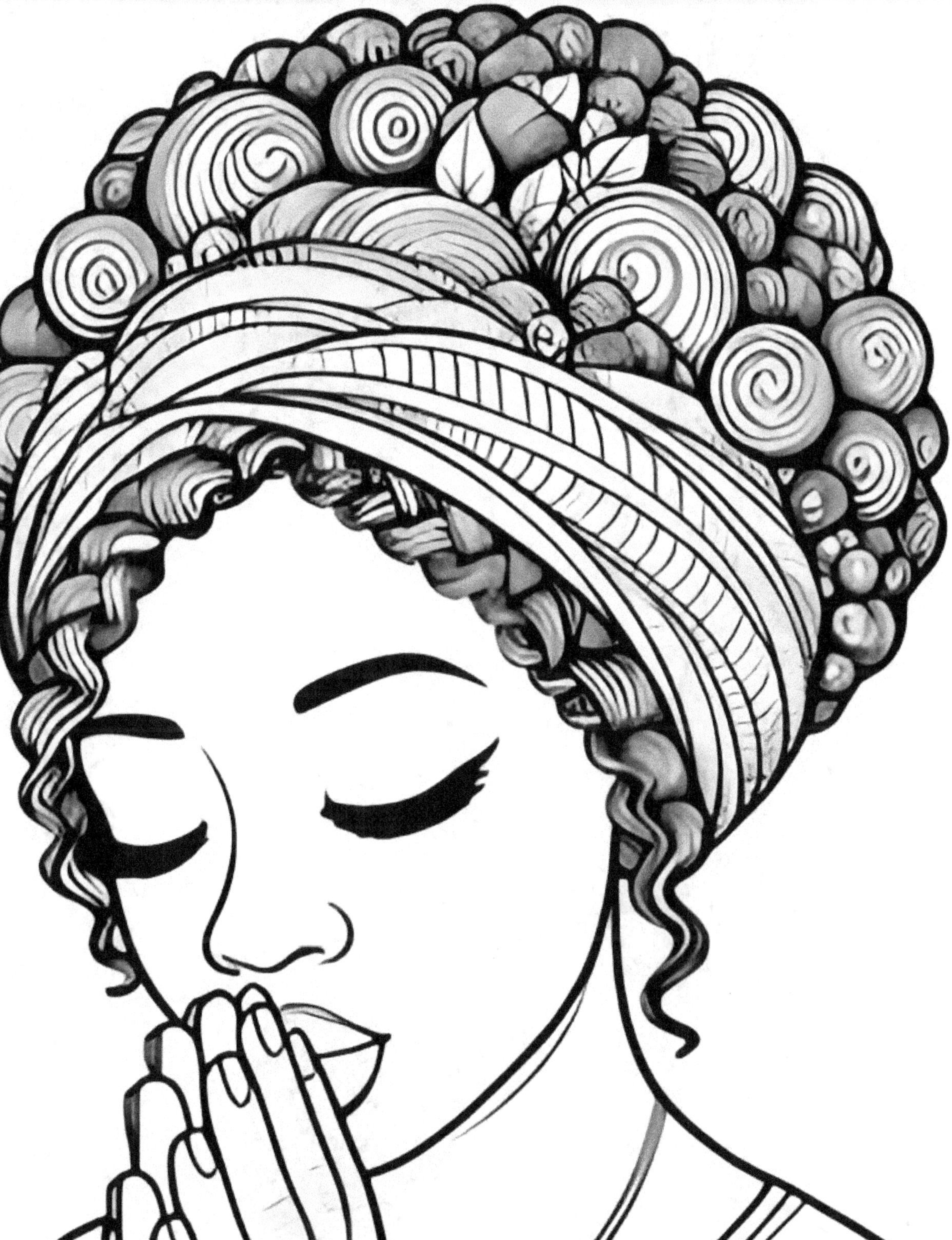

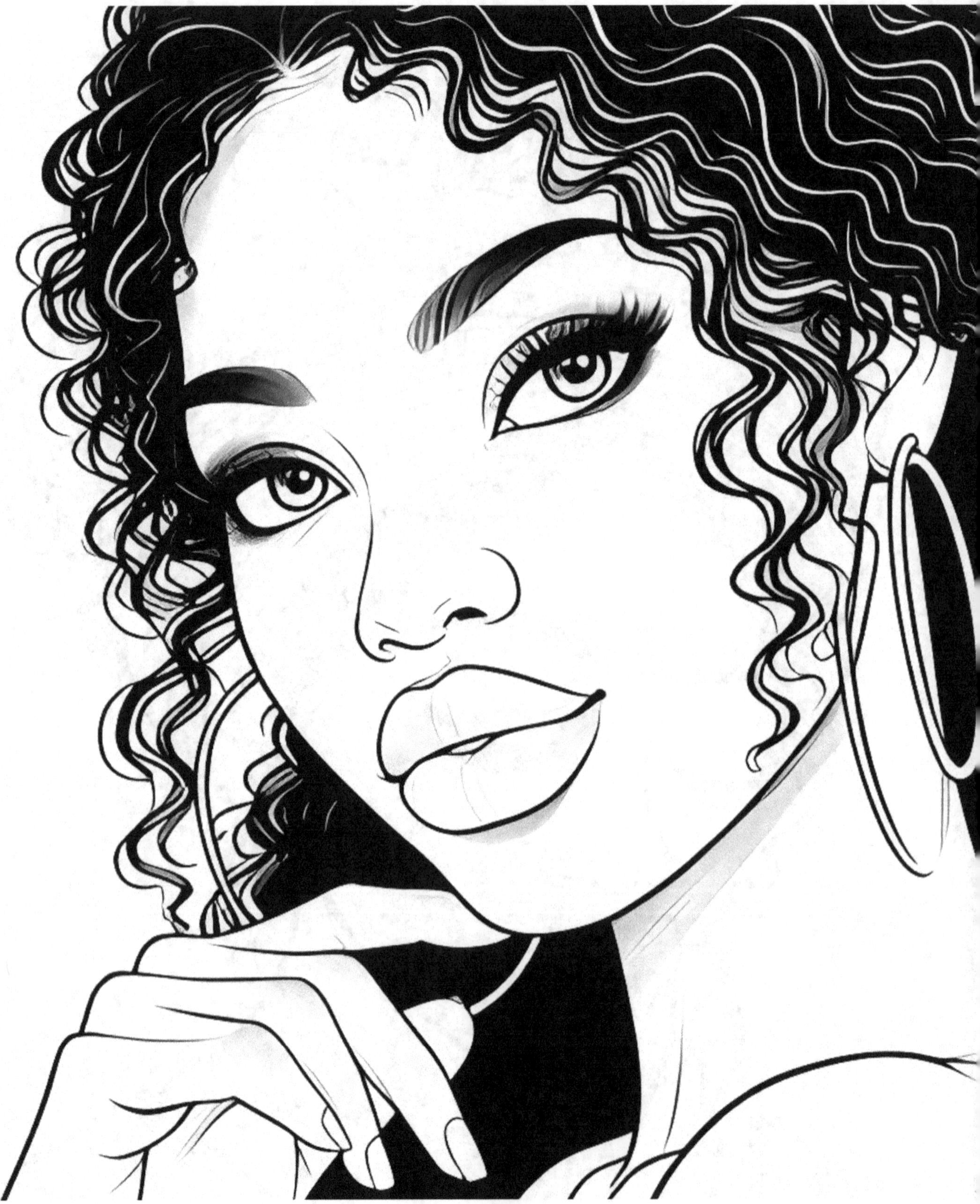

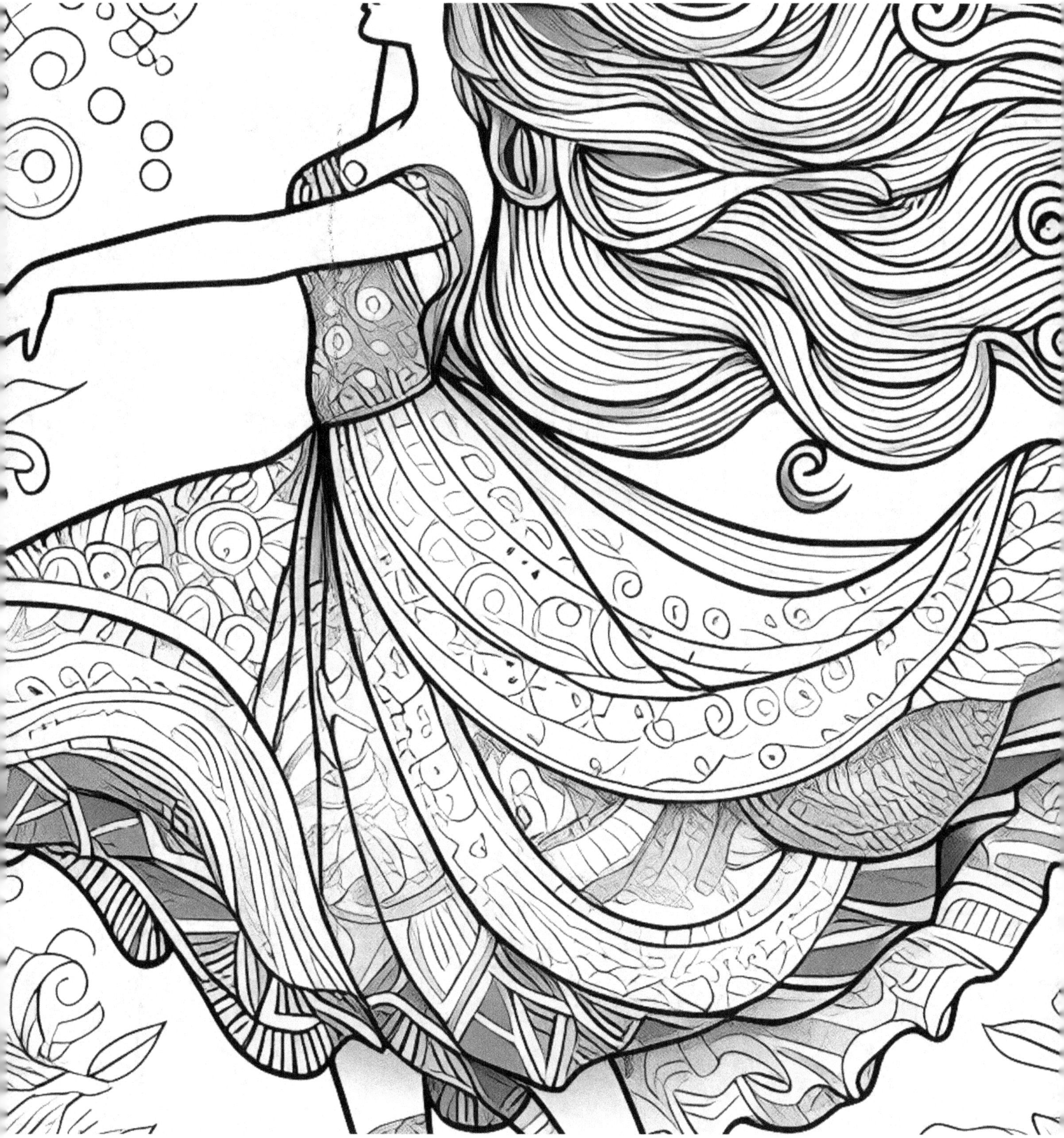

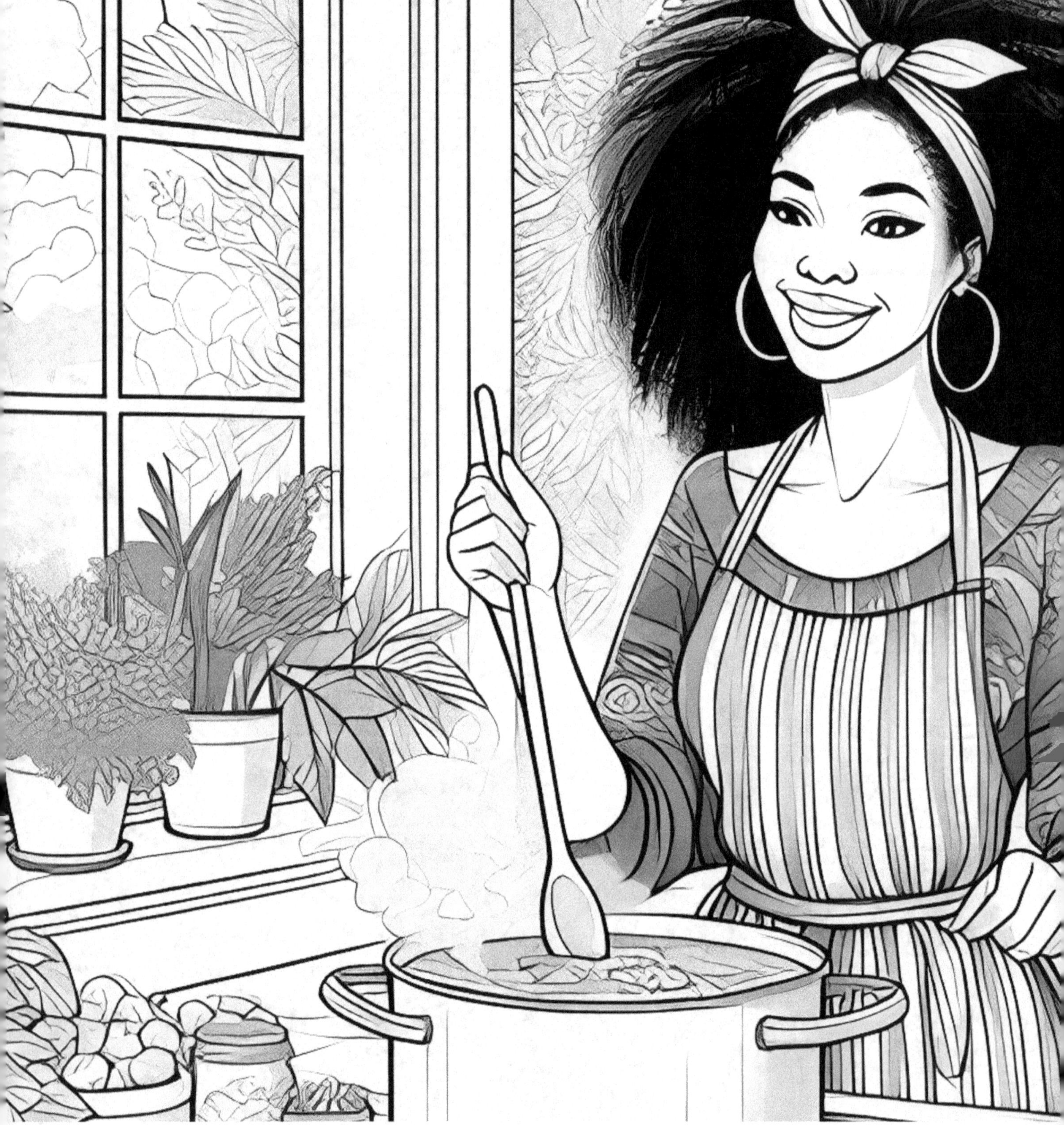

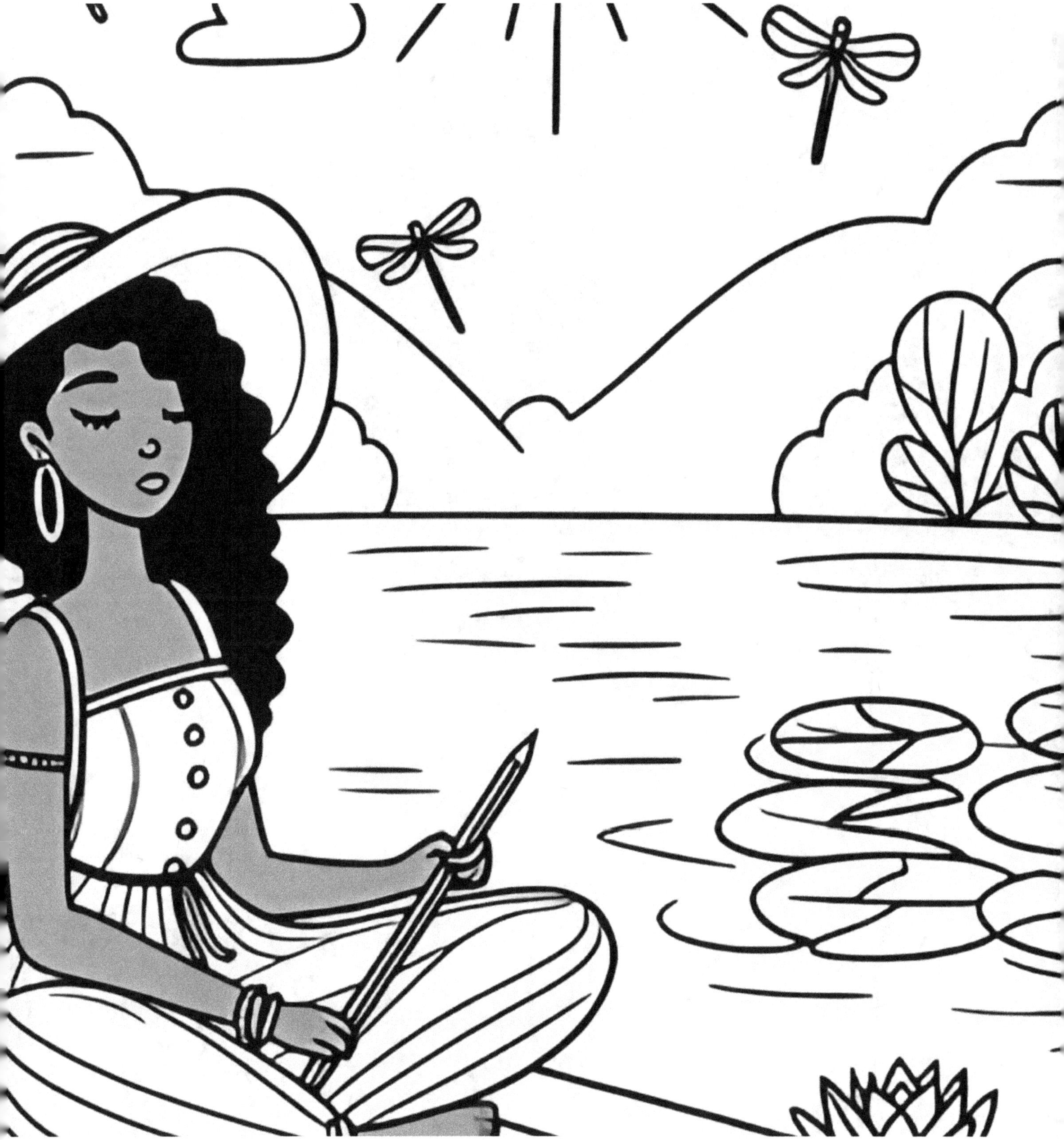

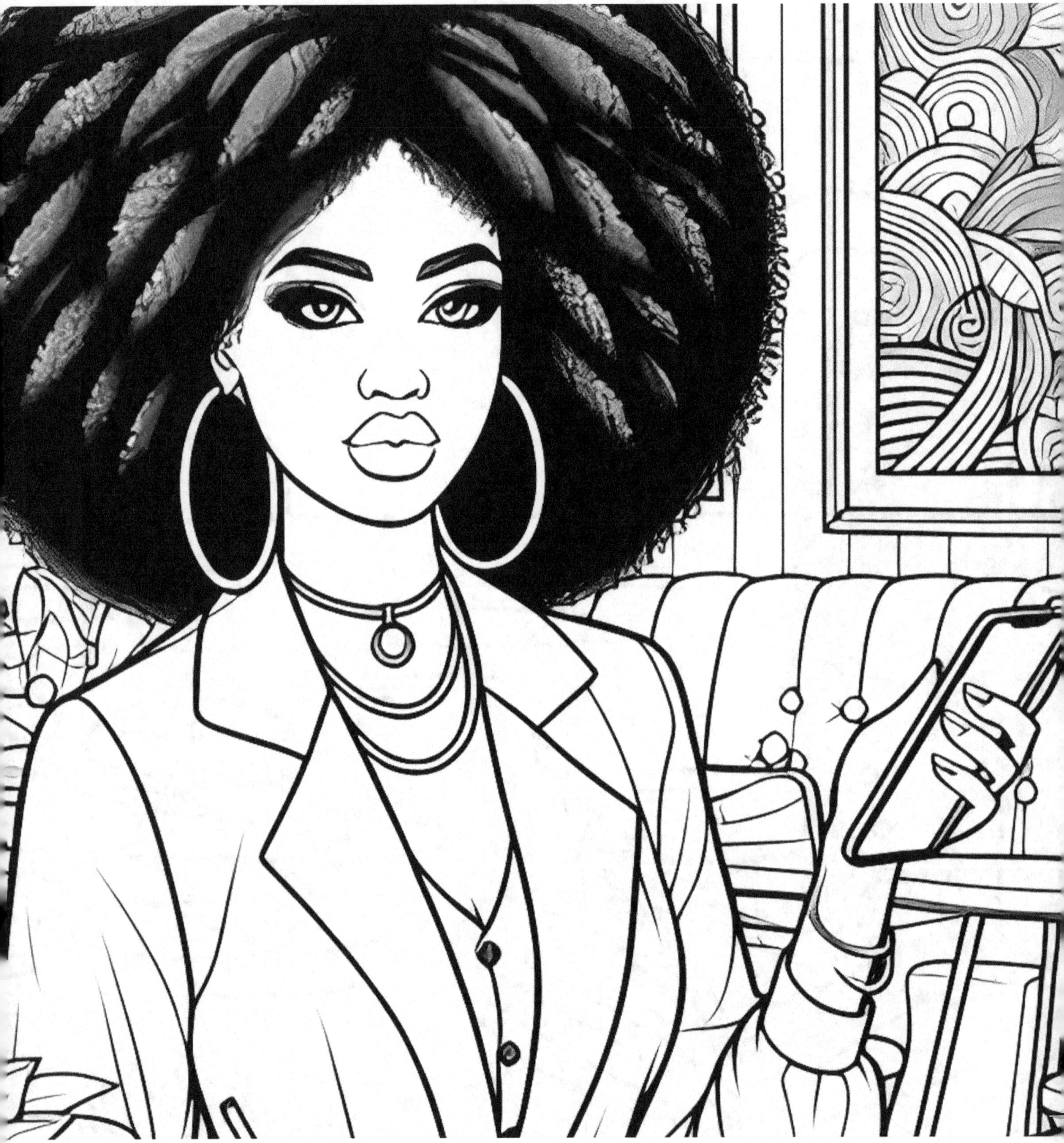

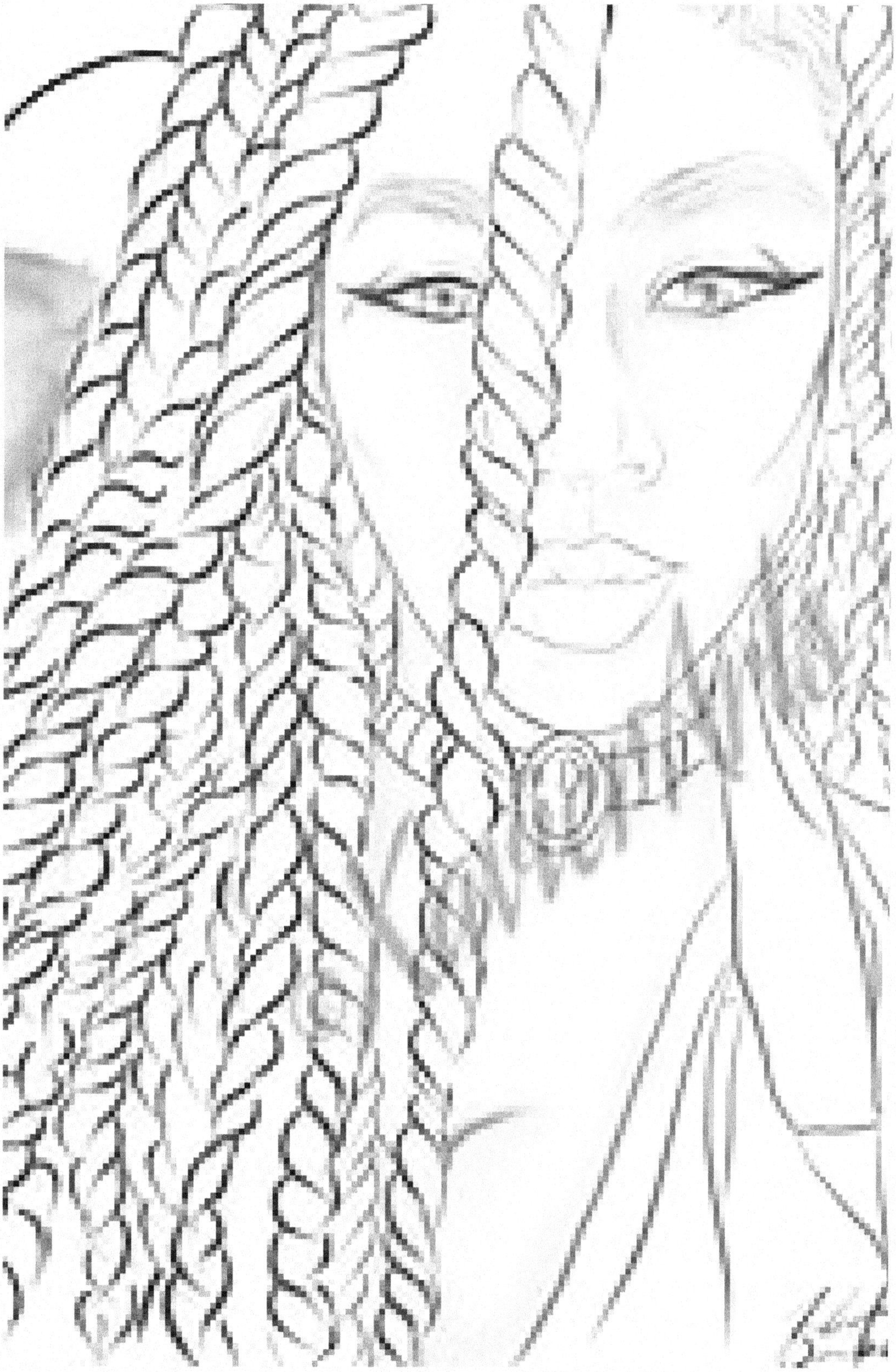

www.ingramcontent.com/pod-product-compliance
Lightning Source LLC
Chambersburg PA
CBHW062238220526
45471CB00009B/3533